D0443098

Tree Frogs

By Erika and Jim Deiters

STECK-VAUGHN
ELEMENTARY · SECONDARY · ADULT · LIBRARY

A Harcourt Company

www.steckvaughn.com

ANIMALS OF THE RAIN FOREST

Library of Congress Cataloging-in-Publication Data is available upon request.

Printed and bound in the United States of America
10 9 8 7 6 5 4 3 2 1 W 04 03 02 01

Photo Acknowledgments
Digital Stock Photos/cover, title page
Root Resources/Anthony Merceica, 8; A.B. Sheldon
Unicorn Stock Photos/Ron Holt, 12
Visuals Unlimited/Joe McDonald, 19, 28; William J. Weber, 11;
    William Palmer, 15; John Serrao; James Beveridge, 22; Nathan W.
    Cohen, 24; Erwin C. "Bud" Nielsen, 26

Contents

UNITED STATES
OF AMERICA

MEXICO

BELIZE
HONDURAS
GUATEMALA   NICARAGUA
EL SALVADOR   *Caribbean Sea*

COSTA RICA
PANAMA
ECUADOR

COLOMBIA

VENEZUELA

North Atlantic Ocean

GUYANA
SURINAME
FRENCH
GUIANA
(FRANCE)

AMAZON
RIVER

PERU

BRAZIL

BOLIVIA

South Pacific Ocean

CHILE

PARAGUAY

South Atlantic Ocean

ARGENTINA   URUGUAY

Range of
the Green
Tree Frog

Range of the
Glass Frog

Surrounding
Land

Water

Borders

Rivers

N
W   E
S

What do tree frogs look like?
Tree frogs have long fingers and toes. They have large eyes. They can be many different colors.

Where do tree frogs live?
Tree frogs live all over the world. More tree frogs live in the rain forests of Central and South America than anywhere else.

What do tree frogs eat?
Tree frogs eat almost any animal they can fit in their mouths. They eat spiders, flies, moths, and worms.

How many kinds of tree frogs are there?
There are over 400 kinds of tree frogs. They are many different sizes. Scientists are still finding new kinds of tree frogs.

The sticky pads on this tree frog's toes
help it hold on to this leaf.

Tree Frogs in Rain Forests

Tree frogs are **amphibians**. Amphibians are animals that live both in the water and on the land. Most amphibians begin their lives in the water. They move to land as adults. Adult tree frogs move from the land into the trees. They have sticky pads on their toes that help them to climb.

Tree frogs and all amphibians are **cold-blooded**. The body temperature of cold-blooded animals is about the same as the air or water around them. Temperature is a measure of heat or cold.

Tree frogs need the heat to warm their bodies. They need to warm their bodies to make their muscles work.

About Tree Frogs

Water is important in the life of tree frogs. They need water to lay eggs in. Water keeps their skin moist. The skin on a tree frog's back legs and stomach soaks up water into its body.

There are over 400 kinds of tree frogs. They are many different sizes and colors. Many are brightly colored. Scientists are still finding new kinds of tree frogs.

Tree frogs are important in nature. They help control the number of insects. Bats, birds, and snakes eat tree frogs. Some snakes eat tree frog eggs.

Where Tree Frogs Live

Tree frogs live all over the world. They need to live in warm and wet places. There are no tree frogs in Antarctica. It is too cold and dry there.

Warm rain forests are perfect homes for tree frogs. The rain forests of Central and

▲ **Frog's bodies soak up water through their skin to keep them moist.**

South America are home to most kinds of tree frogs. Rain forests are places where many trees and plants grow close together and much rain falls. Many different kinds of animals live in rain forests.

▲ This tree frog is sitting among tree leaves.
Its coloring makes it hard to see.

Life in Trees

Most tree frogs live in trees close to water.
They find food in trees. They climb trees to
get away from predators. Predators are
animals that hunt and eat other animals for

food. The animals that predators eat are called prey.

Not all tree frogs live in trees. Some tree frogs make their homes in tall grasses and short bushes. Other tree frogs do not climb at all. The cricket tree frog of North America spends most of its time on the ground in wet areas.

What Tree Frogs Look Like

The most common color for a tree frog is green to blend in with leaves. They also can be blue, red, yellow, orange, and other colors. Some tree frogs have colored markings. A marking is a pattern on an animal. Most tree frogs can change their color to match their backgrounds. They do this to hide from predators.

Tree frogs can be many sizes. Some tree frogs are less than 1 inch (2.5 cm) long. Others are as long as 4.25 inches (11 cm). Female tree frogs may be twice the size of males.

Special Body Parts

Tree frogs have long toes made for climbing. Sticky pads on the ends of their toes help them grip leaves and branches. The White's tree frog is a great climber. It can even climb glass.

Most tree frogs are longer and thinner than other frogs. Their bodies are also flatter. Their different shape gives tree frogs better balance. Balance is the ability to be steady and not fall. Good balance helps them move easily through trees.

Some Kinds of Tree Frogs

The glass frog is an unusual kind of tree frog. It lives in the rain forests of Costa Rica. The skin of this tree frog is transparent. Transparent means it can be seen through. The heart and lungs of the glass frog are visible through its skin.

The rain forests of Central America are home to the red-eyed tree frog. These frogs are known for their large red eyes. Yellow-

▲ **This is a glass frog from the rain forests of Costa Rica.**

eyed tree frogs also live in these rain forests. They are known for their large yellow eyes.

Some tree frogs are nicknamed flying tree frogs. But these frogs do not really fly. They leap into the air and glide. They use their webbed toes to steer. Their sticky toe pads help them land.

This tree frog is eating a moth. Tree frogs eat mainly insects.

Food

Tree frogs will eat any animal that fits in their mouths. They eat ants, caterpillars, spiders, moths, flies, snails, and worms. Tree frogs may also eat fruits and plants.

Tree frogs must be careful about what animals they eat. Many ants in the rain forest can sting. Some rain-forest caterpillars are poisonous. Tree frogs can become sick or die if they eat anything poisonous.

Some tree frogs are picky eaters. Smaller tree frogs may eat only ants or termites. One kind of tree frog in the rain forest of Brazil eats only berries.

Hunting and Eating

Tree frogs look for food at night. They sleep during the day. Tree frogs are hungry when they wake up. They can eat 100 insects in one night.

Tree frogs are good hunters. They climb quietly through branches looking for prey. Tree frogs can see and hear well. Scientists think tree frogs may be able to smell prey. Tree frogs can also feel nearby prey. The smallest movement tells tree frogs where prey is.

Tree frogs move in close once they find prey. They shoot out their sticky tongues to grab prey. A tree frog's tongue can be as long as its head. Their tongues attach to the front of their mouths. Tree frogs have small teeth in their mouths that hold prey.

Tree frogs do not chew their prey. Instead, tree frogs swallow prey whole. Stomach juices then break down whatever the tree frogs have swallowed.

Tree frogs climb plant stems and trees to look for prey.

Tree frog throats fill with air when they call to their mates.

A Tree Frog's Life Cycle

Tree frogs mate at the beginning of the **rainy season**. The rainy season is a time of year when it rains almost every day in the rain forest. Tree frogs need the rain for laying eggs. Males find pools of water and then attract females.

Male tree frogs use special calls to attract females. Large groups of calling males are called a chorus. Each kind of tree frog has a special call. Tree frogs can tell the difference between these calls.

A female red-eyed tree frog laid these eggs on a leaf. Tadpoles grow inside them.

Eggs

The female tries to hide the eggs she lays. Some tree frogs lay dozens of eggs and some lay thousands. Females may hide them in the water. They may place them near grass, behind water plants, or next to rocks.

The eggs hatch after six to eight days. Only a few of the eggs will develop into adult frogs. Fish eat most of the eggs.

Some tree frogs do not need to be in the water to lay eggs. The female red-eyed tree frog lays her eggs on the bottoms of leaves that hang over water. Other kinds of tree frogs lay eggs in water trapped in branches or leaves.

Young

Young tree frogs are called **tadpoles**. Tadpoles look like small fish. They get oxygen through gills. Oxygen is a gas that all animals need in order to live. Gills are body parts that take oxygen from water. Tadpoles and fish get oxygen the same way.

These newly hatched tadpoles are right outside of the egg sac.

Tadpoles

Tadpoles live in water up to 14 weeks. They eat mostly algae. Algae are small rootless plants that grow in water or on damp surfaces.

Tadpoles must look out for predators. Water birds, fish, and snakes eat tadpoles.

Tadpoles change in the water. They begin to grow legs. They grow lungs. They also lose most of their tails.

Tadpoles leave the water as **froglets**. A froglet is a young tree frog with a short tail. The froglet's tail goes back into its body. The tail becomes food for the growing tree frog. After a short time, froglets become adult tree frogs.

The amount of time a tree frog lives depends on what kind it is. Some tree frogs kept as pets can live for 25 years.

This pet tree frog is holding onto its owner's finger.

Living with Tree Frogs

Tree frogs help people. They eat insects. People also use tree frogs to tell the weather. Male tree frogs call for females at the start of the rainy season. People of the rain forest listen for the mating calls. Then they know that rain is coming.

Some people keep tree frogs as pets. Most owners keep tree frogs in glass aquariums filled with leaves and branches. Owners feed tree frogs crickets and mealworms. A mealworm is the **larva** of some kinds of beetles. Larva is the young stage of an insect that looks like a worm.

Tree frogs cannot live in the rain forest if their habitats are taken away.

Medicine

Scientists have found a medicine in the skin of the White's tree frog. The medicine cures cold sores. A cold sore is a kind of sore on a person's face near or in the mouth.

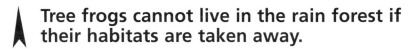

Dying Out

Many tree frogs are dying out. People are cutting down their **habitats**. A habitat is a place where an animal or plant usually lives. People are clearing rain-forest trees to make room for roads and farms. They are also selling the wood. Tree frogs need the safety of leaves and branches. Some kinds of tree frogs may die out before we even know about them.

Tree-frog bodies can be changed by pollution. Pollution is harmful material that is found in air, water, or soil. Pollution thins the air and makes the sun too hot for tree frogs. Tree frog bodies also take in poisons in the water. Scientists are finding tree frogs with extra legs and missing eyes.

Knowing what is harming tree frogs may help people to understand problems with nature. Pollution that changes frogs could affect people in the future. Helping the tree frogs live will also help people.

Glossary

amphibian (am-FIB-ee-uhn)—an animal that begins life in the water and later lives on the land

cold-blooded (KOHLD BLUHD-id)—animals with body temperatures that change according to their surroundings

froglet (FRAWG-lit)—a stage in a frog's growth when it first moves onto land

habitat (HAB-i-tat)—the place where an animal or plant usually lives and grows

larva (LAR-vuh)—the young stage of an insect that looks like a worm

rainy season (RAY-nee SEE-suhn)—a period of time when it rains almost every day in the rain forest; forests and grasslands flood during the rainy season.

tadpole (TAD-pole)—a stage in a frog's growth when it is living in the water

Internet Sites

Nashville Zoo
http://www.nashvillezoo.org/redeye.htm

Pet Library
http://www.petlibrary.com

Rain Forest Alliance
http://www.rainforest-alliance.org

Useful Addresses

Little Wilderness
3030 Mill Street
Reno, NV 89502

Rain Forest Action Network
221 Pine Street, Suite 500
San Francisco, CA 94104

Index